© 1998 Geddes & Grosset Ltd
Published by Geddes & Grosset Ltd,
New Lanark, Scotland.

ISBN 1 85534 832 2

Produced by Simon Girling & Associates,
Hadleigh, Suffolk.

Printed and bound in China.

10 9 8 7 6 5 4 3 2 1

In the
Garden

GEDDES & GROSSET

It was spring. The daffodils in Susie and Sam's garden were waving their sunny yellow heads in the flower borders. In the hedge, two blackbirds were building a nest. Susie, Sam and Mum watched from the kitchen window.

"Look," said Mum. "The mother blackbird has some dried grass in her beak. She must be taking it to the nest."

Sure enough, the little bird disappeared into a hole in the hedge.

"Why is she called a black bird? She's brown!" said Sam.

"The female blackbird is brown, but the male is black all over, apart from his yellow beak," said Mum. "Look! There he is! He's got some twigs for the nest."

The female blackbird popped out of the hedge and flew off. The male bird disappeared inside the hole.

"They're working hard!" said Susie.

"Yes," said Mum. This is a busy time for the birds in the garden. It's a busy time for us too. I must get the vegetable patch ready for planting."

"What are you going to grow?" asked Sam.

"Lots of things," said Mum. "I thought that you and Susie might like to grow some vegetables and flowers too. Would you like that?"

"Yes, please!" said Susie and Sam.

"Let's start your patch right away," said Mum. "Wellington boots on, everybody!"

Outside in the garden, Mum showed Susie and Sam the patch of ground that they could use as their own garden.

"There's no room to grow anything in there," said Susie. "It's full of plants already!"

"Those are weeds," said Mum, "and you two will have to dig them all out!"

Mum gave Susie and Sam a trowel and a fork, and showed them what to do.

"Make sure that you get all the roots out," she said, "or the weeds will grow again."

Susie and Sam set to work, while Mum helped.

"This is hard work!" said Sam after a little while. "Can we stop for a rest?"

"Keep going, Sam. You'll soon be finished. Then we can go and buy some seeds for you to plant," said Mum.

At last, Susie and Sam had removed all the weeds from their special patch of the garden. Mum helped them to dig it all over with a spade to break up the big clumps of soil. Then they raked it smooth.

Just as they finished, a robin appeared and hopped on to the freshly dug soil of the vegetable patch.

"He's looking for worms!" said Mum. "Let's leave him to find his lunch while we go to buy some seeds."

After they had all washed the garden soil from their hands, they set off for the garden centre.

There were so many different kinds of seeds that Susie and Sam did not know what to choose. Mum had to help.

"Let's choose some seeds that grow quickly and some that take a little longer," she said. "We can also choose some plants that will be bright and colourful."

So they bought radish seeds and lettuce seeds that would grow fast and be good to eat. They bought peas, because peas were Susie and Sam's favourite vegetable.

They bought nasturtium seeds because of the brightness of the orange and yellow flowers and they bought a garlic plant.

"What's garlic for?" asked Susie.

"It's delicious in spaghetti sauce," said Mum, "and all sorts of other things. It will take a while for the bulbs to grow, but it will be worth it, you'll see."

"Mmm! Spaghetti!" said Sam, beginning to feel hungry.

It took a long time to get everything planted. They sowed the radish and lettuce seeds in straight rows.

Then they planted the peas, and Mum helped Susie and Sam to put up canes and netting for the pea plants to climb up as they grew.

They took the garlic out of its pot and planted it in a corner. Last of all, Susie and Sam planted the nasturtium seeds around the edge of the patch. Then they gave everything a good watering with the watering can.

"Well done! Soon you will have a garden to be proud of," said Mum.

"All we have to do is wait," said Susie.

"And keep weeding," said Mum.

"How long must we wait?" asked Sam.

"Not too long," said Mum. "If you keep on watering and weeding, we will have radishes and lettuces for our salad in a few weeks' time."

"Then peas and flowers!" said Susie.

"And then garlic for our spaghetti!" said Sam. "What's for dinner? Gardening makes me hungry!"

Mum led the way back inside.

Susie and Sam had finished work for the day, but outside the blackbirds kept busy until dark. Soon the female bird would be laying her eggs in the nest. Spring was a very busy time indeed!